PUERTO RICANS IN AMERICA

web enhanced at www.inamericabooks.com

STACY TAUS-BOLSTAD

LERNER PUBLICATIONS COMPANY / MINNEAPOLIS

⇨ Current information and statistics quickly become out of date. That's why we developed **www.inamericabooks.com**, a companion website to the **In America** series. The site offers lots of additional information—downloadable photos and maps and up-to-date facts through links to additional websites. Each link has been carefully selected by researchers at Lerner Publishing Group and is regularly reviewed and updated. However, Lerner Publishing Group is not responsible for the accuracy or suitability of material on websites that are not maintained directly by us. It is recommended that students using the Internet be supervised by a parent, a librarian, a teacher, or other adult.

Lerner Publications Company
A division of Lerner Publishing Group
241 First Avenue North
Minneapolis, MN 55401 U.S.A.

Website address: www.lernerbooks.com

Library of Congress Cataloging-in-Publication Data

Taus-Bolstad, Stacy.
    Puerto Ricans in America / by Stacy Taus-Bolstad.
        p.   cm. — (In America)
    Summary: Examines the history of Puerto Rican immigration to the United States mainland, discussing why Puerto Ricans come, what their lives are like after they arrive, where they settle, and customs they bring from home.
    Includes bibliographical references and index.
    ISBN: 0–8225–3953–5 (lib. bdg. : alk. paper)
    1. Puerto Ricans—United States—History—Juvenile literature. 2. Puerto Ricans—United States—Juvenile literature. [1. Puerto Ricans—United States.] I. Title. II. Series: In America (Minneapolis, Minn.)
E184.P85T38 2005
304.8'7307295—dc22   2003022690

Manufactured in the United States of America
1 2 3 4 5 6 – JR – 10 09 08 07 06 05

CONTENTS

INTRODUCTION 4
Puerto Ricans in America

1 • IN PUERTO RICO 6
The First Inhabitants
Spanish Colony
Toward Independence
A U.S. Possession

2 • MOVING TO THE MAINLAND. . 22
Land of Problems
Making a Living
Learning Curve
Family Matters
Walking the Poverty Line
United They Stand

3 • MAKING THEIR MARK. 40
El Barrio
Identity Crisis
Nuyoricans
A Growing Voice
Making Changes
Forging Ahead

FAMOUS PUERTO RICAN AMERICANS . . 58
TIMELINE 62
GLOSSARY 64
THINGS TO SEE AND DO 64
SOURCE NOTES 66
SELECTED BIBLIOGRAPHY 66
FURTHER READING AND WEBSITES . . 68
INDEX 70

INTRODUCTION

In America, a walk down a city street can seem like a walk through many lands. Grocery stores sell international foods. Shops offer products from around the world. People strolling past may speak foreign languages. This unique blend of cultures is the result of America's history as a nation of immigrants.

Native peoples have lived in North America for centuries. The next settlers were the Vikings. In about A.D. 1000, they sailed from Scandinavia to lands that would become Canada, Greenland, and Iceland. In 1492 the Italian navigator Christopher Columbus landed in the Americas, and more European explorers arrived during the 1500s. In the 1600s, British settlers formed colonies that, after the Revolutionary War (1775–1783), would become the United States. And in the mid-1800s, a great wave of immigration brought millions of new arrivals to the young country.

Immigrants have many different reasons for leaving home. They may leave to escape poverty, war, or harsh governments. They may want better living conditions for themselves and their children. Throughout its history, America has been known as a nation that offers many opportunities. For this reason, many immigrants come to America.

Moving to a new country is not easy. It can mean making a long, difficult journey. It means leaving home and starting over in an unfamiliar place. But it also means using skill, talent, and determination to build a new life. The In America series tells the story of immigration to the United States and the search for fresh beginnings in a new country—in America.

PUERTO RICANS IN AMERICA

Puerto Ricans began moving to the United States in small numbers during the late 1800s to escape political and economic problems in their island homeland. This small trickle steadily increased over the following decades, especially after the Jones Act made Puerto Ricans U.S. citizens in 1917. Many more Puerto Ricans moved to the mainland United States, looking for better jobs.

The biggest wave of Puerto Rican migrants started in the 1940s and 1950s. This mass migration was due to the island's deteriorating economy and a dramatic population increase. These factors left many Puerto Ricans unemployed and homeless. As a result, hundreds of thousands of Puerto Ricans looked to the mainland for hope and opportunity.

But moving to the mainland presented new problems for the migrants. They faced language barriers, poor housing, and discrimination. They struggled to find jobs, and more importantly, they struggled to fit into their new society while maintaining their own identity.

As Puerto Rican Americans moved back and forth between the island and the mainland, they soon began reshaping both places. They brought Puerto Rican culture to the mainland United States and also brought mainland ideas to the island. Puerto Rican Americans have made important contributions to the mainland United States in many ways. They are entertainers, businesspeople, athletes, politicians, and leaders.

By 2000 more than 3.4 million Puerto Ricans lived in the mainland United States. Puerto Rican Americans continue to be an important and growing influence in America—in politics, business, arts, and culture.

1 IN PUERTO RICO

Puerto Rico is an island located about one thousand miles southeast of Miami, Florida. Puerto Rico is part of a chain of islands that stretches from Florida to the South American country of Venezuela. This island chain, known as the West Indies, encloses the Caribbean Sea, an arm of the Atlantic Ocean. Because the island lies at one of the main passageways between the Atlantic and the Caribbean Sea, Puerto Rico has earned the nickname the "Crossroads of the Caribbean."

Puerto Rico is made up of a large rectangular island called Puerto Rico and several smaller islands. The three largest of these are Mona, Culebra, and Vieques. The main island of Puerto Rico, which is about 110 miles east to west and 35 miles north to south, is about the same size as the state of Connecticut. The island has rich

Pristine beaches, lush vegetation, and plenty of sunshine have lured visitors to Puerto Rico for years.

soil, a warm climate, and plenty of sunshine and rain. Tropical flowers and fruit–bearing trees cover Puerto Rico. The national anthem of Puerto Rico describes the island as a "flowering garden of magical beauty."

Puerto Rico is a commonwealth of the United States. This means that Puerto Rico governs itself, but the United States has a say in the political and economic affairs of the island. Puerto Ricans are citizens of the United States. They may move freely between the island and the mainland, though they may not vote in U.S. presidential elections and are not required to pay U.S. taxes.

THE FIRST INHABITANTS

The earliest inhabitants of Puerto Rico settled the island between two thousand and four thousand years ago. Historians know very little about this early group, but they probably came on rafts from North America.

Another group, known as the Arawak, settled on the island sometime between 400 B.C. and A.D. 100. The Arawak probably came from South America. They fished, hunted game with bows and arrows, and gathered fruits and berries. The Arawak also created high-quality clay pots and stone tools. This group made Puerto Rico their home until about A.D. 600, when they disappeared from the island. Scientists disagree about why the Arawak left the island. Some scientists believe that other groups chased the Arawak off the island or that disease wiped out their population. Others believe that the Arawak married different groups living in the Caribbean and eventually developed a new culture.

TO FIND OUT MORE INFORMATION ON PUERTO RICAN HISTORY, CULTURE, AND PEOPLE, VISIT WWW.INAMERICABOOKS.COM FOR LINKS.

These rock carvings are among what little evidence remains of the Arawak presence on the island.

By A.D. 1000 another group, called the Taino, were living on the island. The Taino called their home Boriquén, or "land of the valiant one." Taino men fished and hunted, and Taino women gathered berries, pineapples, and other tropical fruits. They also farmed. They planted corn, peanuts, sweet potatoes, and other crops. The Taino were skilled builders and sailors. Taino villages were usually located in valleys, where soil was fertile. Most villages consisted of simple huts. The largest hut belonged to the *cacique*, or chief. The cacique governed village affairs, and his word was law.

The Taino believed that spirits and gods controlled everything in nature, including plants and animals, the earth and the sky, the sun and the rain. They honored these spirits with prayers and offerings. One god that the Taino could not please, however, was Huracán, the god of evil. Huracán was believed to bring terrible

The Taino constructed their simple huts out of the trunks of palm trees.

winds to the island every fall. These winds are called hurricanes.

The Taino were peaceful people. In fact, the word *taino* means "gentle." But their peaceful way of life was continually threatened by a neighboring group of people called the Carib. By the 1400s, the Carib had settled on nearby islands and frequently attacked the Taino. The Carib destroyed Taino villages and took Taino women. Because the Carib dominated the West Indies, the area became known as the

Caribbean. By the late 1400s, however, the Taino faced an even greater threat than the fierce Carib—Spain.

SPANISH COLONY

In 1492 an Italian explorer named Christopher Columbus set sail from Spain, hoping to find a new route from Europe to Asia. Instead, Columbus landed in the Americas. When Columbus returned to Spain in 1493, Spain's royal family immediately sponsored a second trip to further explore this New World. Columbus set sail for the Caribbean.

Columbus reached Boriquén on November 19, 1493. Impressed with the beautiful island, he claimed it for Spain. He named the island San Juan Bautista, after Saint John the Baptist. Then he sailed away and left the island in peace. Spain ignored San Juan Bautista for fifteen years. But in 1508, a Spanish nobleman named Ponce de León arrived with fifty men to explore and settle on the island. When Ponce de León and his men

Christopher Columbus (holding flag) *claimed Puerto Rico, then known as Boriquén, for Spain in 1493. Columbus decided to rename the island in honor of a Christian saint.*

Ponce de León settled on Puerto Rico in 1508, becoming the island's first governor.

AY, QUE PUERTO RICO! (OH, WHAT A RICH PORT!)

—*Ponce de León, on seeing Puerto Rico's bay for the first time*

landed on the island, the friendly Taino greeted them. The Taino helped the Spaniards build their settlement, which they named Caparra. Ponce de León also renamed the island Puerto Rico, or "rich port" in Spanish.

Ponce de León became the island's first governor. His main goal on Puerto Rico was to establish a Spanish colony, or settlement. The Spaniards soon discovered gold in the island's rivers and streams. The well-armed Spanish colonists forced the Taino to dig for gold. Soon the first mines opened on the island's north coast.

The colonists quickly used up the small gold supply, however. They then turned to farming for their livelihood. The island's mild climate was perfect for profitable crops such as sugar and coffee. The Spaniards forced the Taino to plant and harvest the colonists' crops and to build roads and houses.

This forced labor killed many Taino. Others died of diseases, such as yellow fever, that the Spaniards carried with them to the islands. While the Taino wanted to fight back to rid the island of the Spanish, their stone axes were little match for the Spaniards' guns and swords. Even so, in 1511, after the Taino's pleas for better treatment were ignored, the Taino rebelled. Spanish

MAP MIX UP?

The origin of Puerto Rico's name is a bit of a mystery. Columbus originally named the island San Juan Bautista, in honor of Saint John the Baptist. According to legend, Ponce de León nicknamed one of its first settlements Puerto Rico, or "rich port." So how did the two switch names? Some historians believe that an early mapmaker simply made a mistake and labeled the island Puerto Rico and the town San Juan.

soldiers shot more than six thousand Taino. Many Taino survivors fled to the mountains or joined their former enemies, the Caribs. But a few Taino stayed on Puerto Rico and married Spanish settlers.

Without the Taino to work in the fields and the mines, the Spanish settlers wanted a new source of cheap labor. Ponce de León begged Spain's King Ferdinand V for permission to bring African slaves to Puerto Rico. In 1513 the first shipload of African slaves arrived on the island. But with the slaves came a terrible disease called smallpox. This disease further reduced the already shrinking Taino population.

By the 1530s, colonists had stripped Puerto Rico of nearly all its gold. More and more Spaniards turned to agriculture for their livelihood. Sugarcane soon became the island's most important crop. Despite the island's increased workforce, however, many problems continued to plague Puerto Rico. The African slaves attempted many rebellions to protest the harsh treatment they received. And the Spanish government allowed the colonists to trade only with Spain, making it difficult for the Puerto Rican settlers to turn a profit. In addition, hurricanes, diseases, and Carib attacks plagued the island.

Although Puerto Rico failed as a source of profit for Spain, the Spanish king recognized the island's importance as a military and trading post. As Spain conquered more areas in the Americas, the Puerto Rican city of San Juan became an important port for Spanish ships. San Juan grew as Spanish ships carrying gold and silver from South American countries stopped at the island for supplies and repairs.

France, Great Britain, and the Netherlands also saw the island as a valuable port. They wanted to weaken Spain's power in the West Indies and in the Americas. In the late 1500s and early 1600s, the French, British, and Dutch all repeatedly attacked Puerto Rico. The

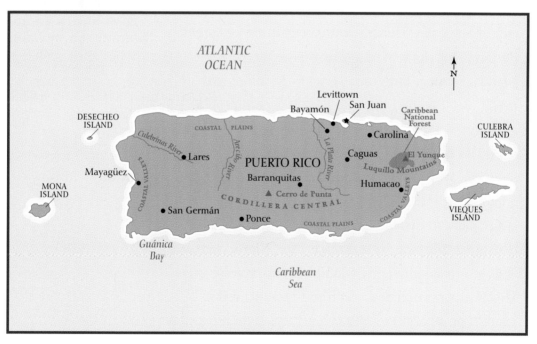

The "island" of Puerto Rico is actually several islands. Though small in size, the main island of Puerto Rico is one of the most densely populated areas in the world. Download this and other maps at www.inamericabooks.com.

Spanish built several fortresses to protect their colony. By 1625 Spain had driven away these attackers.

Even so, Spain lost much of its power in the Caribbean during the 1600s. Fewer Spanish supply ships stopped at the island, hurting the local economy. Colonists suffered from food and textile shortages. Puerto Rican colonists began trading illegally with the British, French, and Dutch. Spanish officials who were supposed to keep foreign traders off of the island also traded with many of them.

During this time, intermarriage between the island's three main ethnic groups—Taino, Spanish, and African—became more common. Spanish–Taino and Spanish–African people began to populate the city of San Juan. This blending of cultures reshaped Puerto Rico's society. Taino words peppered the island's Spanish language. African traditions and music also blended into the Puerto Rican lifestyle.

TO LEARN MORE ABOUT THE INFLUENCE OF GROUPS SUCH AS THE TAINO, THE AFRICANS, AND THE SPANISH ON PUERTO RICAN CULTURE, CHECK OUT WWW.INAMERICABOOKS.COM FOR LINKS.

Because Puerto Rico was not allowed to trade with countries other than Spain, it remained poor during the early 1700s. To help improve the island's economy, Spain gathered up small farms and turned them into sugar plantations. Coffee, tobacco, and cotton also became important farm products for Puerto Rico. As agriculture boomed, the island's economy also grew. This in turn brought about rapid growth in the island's population as Spanish settlers took advantage of the government's offer of free land. The increased population made it profitable for trading ships to stop on the island, which further bolstered the economy.

New towns soon sprang up around the island.

TOWARD INDEPENDENCE

Spain began losing control of its colonies during the early 1800s. Frequent wars with French and British forces over European and American territories weakened an already suffering Spanish government. Because of this, Spain did not have enough troops to control its colonies, including Puerto Rico.

Many Puerto Ricans were unhappy with Spain. Puerto Rican farmers, called *jibaros*, were forced to work on the larger plantations. Many jibaros lived in poverty and wanted their lands back from the Spanish plantation owners. Many Puerto Ricans also opposed slavery,

JIBAROS

Jibaros were Puerto Rican peasant farmers. Many were descendants of runaway Taino and African slaves or of Spanish deserters. They usually lived in the mountains and countryside of Puerto Rico. Few jibaros attended school, and they spent their days working in the fields.

Few modern Puerto Ricans live as jibaros, but many Puerto Ricans view jibaros as folk heroes. They represent the island's past and its independent lifestyle.

demanding that Spain free the African slaves on the island. Spanish plantation owners and business owners also wanted more freedom. They paid high taxes and were not allowed to trade with countries other than Spain. Most Puerto Ricans wanted better schools and hospitals, more roads and businesses, and a say in the island's government.

Spain was too involved with its own political problems to deal effectively with Puerto Rico's demands. Spain promised reforms that would give Puerto Rico greater freedom and control over its own affairs. But Spain often failed to keep its promises. Puerto Rico enjoyed some very brief periods of increased political freedom. But these periods were followed by long stretches of absolute rule by Spanish governors. One important reform the Spanish king did make was in 1815, when the government opened Puerto Rico's ports to trade with any nation.

Ramón Emeterio Betances was a medical doctor before he became known as the revolutionary behind Puerto Rico's independence movement.

By 1868 Puerto Ricans had grown tired of waiting for Spain to act. One group, led by Ramón Emeterio Betances, believed the time had come to declare Puerto Rico's independence. On September 23, 1868, Betances's followers marched into the small town of Lares and captured the town hall. Raising banners with the words "Liberty or Death!" they proclaimed the birth of the Republic of Puerto Rico. But Spain quickly put down the uprising, killing or capturing many of the rebels.

Those Puerto Rican rebels who escaped Spain's punishment were forced to leave their homeland after the uprising. The promise of more freedom and higher wages led many of these early migrants to the United States. For these early migrants, New York City became their final destination. Most found work in the city's Latino-owned cigar factories. Others found work as sailors or garment markers. Some came to study at the country's colleges.

For these early Puerto Rican Americans, their homeland's independence remained an important social cause. They formed political clubs to help determine the island's status when it gained its freedom from Spain.

Finally, in 1897 Spain granted Puerto Rico the power to elect a congress that shared power with a governor appointed by Spain. In 1898 Luis Muñoz Rivera became the leader of the new Puerto Rican government. Puerto Ricans finally had a say in their nation's government.

When Puerto Ricans finally won the right to elect their own officials, they selected Luis Muñoz Rivera as their new leader.

A U.S. POSSESSION

Puerto Rico's new government was short-lived, however. In 1898 the United States and Spain began fighting the Spanish–American War. The United States wanted to force Spain out of the Caribbean. U.S. troops landed at Puerto Rico's Guánica Bay. They met little resistance from the Puerto Ricans, who hoped that the United States would ensure democracy and prosperity for their island.

On October 18, 1898, General John R. Brooke became the first U.S. military governor of Puerto Rico. Spain signed a treaty on December 10, 1898, to end the war and officially gave Puerto Rico, Cuba, and the Philippines to the United States.

The U.S. military established a temporary government in Puerto Rico that lasted for two years. Puerto Ricans once again had little say in their government. In 1900 the U.S. Congress established the Foraker Act, which established a civilian (non–military) government on the island. But Puerto Ricans, who were not U.S. citizens, had little say in the governing process. While the Puerto Ricans could elect some lower-level politicians, the U.S. president kept the right to appoint the governor and upper-level officials. A resident commissioner from Puerto Rico was sent to Washington, D.C. The resident commissioner could speak to the U.S. Congress on Puerto Rican affairs but had no vote. In some ways, the Puerto

We have not come to make war upon the people of a country that for centuries has been oppressed but on the contrary to bring you protection . . . to promote your prosperity and to bestow upon you the . . . blessings of the liberal institutions of our government.

—General Nelson Miles, in his first public speech as military governor of Puerto Rico

Ricans received less freedom to govern themselves under U.S. rule than they had under Spanish rule.

The United States worked to build the island's economy. At the time, many of the 900,000 people living on Puerto Rico were poor plantation workers. Most lived in huts. Only one out of ten children attended school. The United States also established free trade between the island and the United States—a big advantage for Puerto Rico.

Puerto Rico experienced economic expansion due partly to increased trade with the United States. The U.S. government funded roads, dams, hospitals, and schools on the island. Many U.S. businesses moved their factories to the island. U.S. businesses invested in Puerto Rico's rich farmland. They took over Spanish plantations and bought up the remaining small sugar fields from independent farmers to combine them, forming a few giant corporations. This action gave Puerto Rico's economy a dramatic boost. But it also hurt many of the island's farmers.

Though the island's economy thrived, most Puerto Rican workers still lived in poverty. Companies paid their workers low wages to help increase the profits for the owners. And the work was seasonal, so many Puerto Ricans were out of work for part of the year. Puerto Ricans believed that nothing would change until they could govern themselves.

In 1917 the U.S. Congress passed the Jones Act. This act defined Puerto Rico as an "organized but unincorporated" territory of the United States. This meant that Puerto Ricans became citizens of the United States. This act also gave the islanders the right to elect officials to government.

The Jones Act had some problems. Puerto Ricans had a say in their government, but the major power remained with the U.S. president. The president still appointed the island's governor. The act also failed to

FIND LINKS TO LEARN MORE ABOUT U.S. AND PUERTO RICAN HISTORY AT WWW.INAMERICABOOKS.COM.

Low wages, high prices on consumer goods, and a quickly growing population forced many Puerto Ricans to crowd into filthy slums such as this one during the early 1900s.

address the extreme poverty that the majority of Puerto Rican people still faced. Workers received some of the lowest wages in the Caribbean. Yet prices for necessities such as food and clothing—many of which were imported from the mainland—were very high.

All of these factors took their toll on the island. By the 1920s, Puerto Rico was nicknamed the Poorhouse of the Caribbean. Making matters worse, the island's population was growing faster than ever before. Rural families frequently had ten or more children. Better health care kept people alive longer. By 1925 the island was one of the most densely populated areas in the entire world. People left the countryside looking for work in the cities' factories. The cities soon faced housing shortages as the population swelled.

Because of these problems, Puerto Ricans began migrating to the mainland in large numbers. Since Puerto Ricans were citizens of the United States, immigration laws did not apply to them. They were considered migrants, not immigrants. They traveled freely between the island of Puerto Rico and the mainland United States. While most of the migrants settled in New York—the most common port of entry for boats from Puerto Rico—others settled in Chicago, Boston, New Orleans, and Miami. Some even moved as far west as California.

Natural disaster also forced people to leave their homeland at this time. Two hurricanes—one in 1928 and one in 1930—devastated the island. Hundreds of people died, and thousands were suddenly homeless. The island's plantations lay in ruin. Unemployment skyrocketed, and islanders dealt with hunger, poor housing, and disease. This in turn led to violence. Riots broke out in 1936 and 1937 as unemployment and starvation continued to trouble the island. More and more Puerto Ricans turned to the mainland. They believed they could make a better life for themselves and their families in America.

MANY PEOPLE ARE INTERESTED IN LEARNING ABOUT THEIR FAMILY'S HISTORY. THIS STUDY IS CALLED GENEALOGY. IF YOU'D LIKE TO LEARN ABOUT YOUR OWN GENEALOGY AND HOW YOUR ANCESTORS CAME TO AMERICA, VISIT WWW.INAMERICABOOKS.COM FOR TIPS AND LINKS TO HELP YOU GET STARTED.

2

MOVING TO THE MAINLAND

World War II (1939–1945) was a turning point for Puerto Ricans. About sixty-five thousand Puerto Ricans served in the U.S. military in the fight against Germany and the Axis powers of Italy and Japan. Because of this service, many Americans supported the Puerto Ricans' self-government movement. In 1947, after years of fighting for self-rule, Puerto Ricans gained the power to elect their own governor. Luis Muñoz Marín became governor of Puerto Rico.

Despite political advances, the most important period of Puerto Rican migration to the continental United States was under way at this time. Several factors encouraged this migration to the mainland. Puerto Rico's economy, still weak and underdeveloped, kept many people in extreme poverty. In addition, the problems of overpopulation and underemployment remained unresolved.

The war had limited the production of popular consumer goods, such as refrigerators and clothing. After World War II, the United States needed workers for its booming new factories and plants. Mainland businesses paid higher wages than Puerto Rican factories and farms. To ease unemployment and overpopulation, both the Puerto Rican and the U.S. government encouraged people to migrate to the United States. Billboards in San Juan and other major cities urged people to move to New York City. The government also agreed to help pay many migrants' fares.

TO DISCOVER SOME OF THE MANY STORIES OF PUERTO RICANS MIGRATING TO THE UNITED STATES, VISIT WWW.INAMERICABOOKS.COM FOR LINKS.

Many migrants believed that America was the land of opportunity. Since many Puerto Ricans had trained or had been stationed on the mainland during World War II, they had seen mainland prosperity firsthand. Jobs on the mainland were plentiful and living

OPERATION BOOTSTRAP

In 1947 the Puerto Rican government started a program called Operation Bootstrap. The program worked to improve the island's economy. Through the program, the government supplied electricity to factories and offered loans to new businesses. It also encouraged foreign investment and brought foreign companies to Puerto Rico. This in turn created jobs for more Puerto Ricans. Operation Bootstrap made manufacturing Puerto Rico's most important industry.

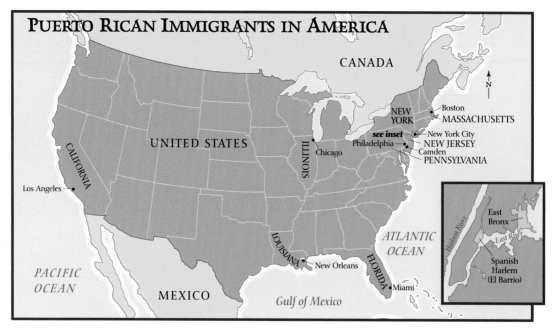

Puerto Rican Immigrants in America

CANADA

NEW YORK
Boston
MASSACHUSETTS

see inset
New York City
Philadelphia
NEW JERSEY
Camden
PENNSYLVANIA

UNITED STATES

ILLINOIS

Chicago

CALIFORNIA

Los Angeles

LOUISIANA

New Orleans

FLORIDA

Miami

ATLANTIC
OCEAN

PACIFIC
OCEAN

MEXICO

Gulf of Mexico

N

Hudson River

East
Bronx

East River

Spanish
Harlem
(El Barrio)

*Though a majority of Puerto Ricans have settled in New York City, especially in El Barrio
and the East Bronx (inset), there are also large Puerto Rican populations in Chicago,
Miami, Boston, and New Orleans. Visit www.inamericabooks.com to download this map.*

conditions seemed rich. Since Puerto Ricans could travel freely between the island and the mainland, many believed they would make their fortunes in America and later return to the island.

Another reason for the mass migration from the island to the mainland was that air transportation expanded rapidly after the war. This made the trip from San Juan to New York City short and relatively cheap. Airplane tickets cost less than fifty dollars by the end of the 1940s. Thousands of Puerto Ricans came to the mainland by plane. While the majority of Puerto Ricans lived in New York, large Puerto Rican communities also developed in New Jersey, Massachusetts, Pennsylvania, Florida, California, and Illinois.

The Puerto Rican government soon realized the need for an organization that would help new migrants. In 1948 the Puerto Rican government opened the Office of the Commonwealth in New York City. The office helped migrants find work and understand city services. It worked to pass laws to protect the rights of seasonal farmworkers, who were often paid poorly. Regional offices soon opened in Chicago and Camden, New Jersey, as the migrant populations in those cities grew.

Puerto Ricans also created aid societies, called *hermandades* (brotherhoods, in Spanish). Hermandades served as social clubs as well as offered financial aid and medical care to Puerto Rican communities. Hermandades also provided a center for weddings and other community celebrations, including holidays.

Greater numbers of islanders came to the mainland after 1950. Even though the U.S. Congress approved the Puerto Rican Constitution and established the Commonwealth of Puerto Rico in

The promise of higher wages, better living conditions, and cheap airfare prompted many Puerto Rican laborers to move to the mainland after World War II.

1952, the mass migrations continued. In 1953, the year in which the largest number of Puerto Ricans came to the mainland, migration reached almost 70,000 people in one year. By the mid-1950s, while the island's population reached 2.2 million, about 675,000 Puerto Ricans lived on the mainland. Because most Puerto Rican migrants were concentrated in New York City, many mainlanders nicknamed the city the "Puerto Rican capital of the world."

LAND OF PROBLEMS

America did not always prove to be the land of opportunity for the many Puerto Rican migrants who made the trip. Most Puerto Ricans who migrated to New York received a cold greeting—literally. Used to Puerto Rico's warm and sunny climate, many migrants found themselves unprepared to deal with the cold and dark northern winters. Many had never even seen snow. While they quickly learned to adapt to the cool climate, the cool reception they received from mainlanders made the Puerto Ricans feel unwelcome. The expression *"¡Hace mucho frío!"* (It's very cold!) often referred to more than just the weather.

Many Americans at this time discriminated against people of African, Asian, or Native American

Many Puerto Ricans were unprepared for the snowy cold of New York City winters.

heritage. Because many Puerto Rican migrants spoke poor English and had darker skin, they were often discriminated against in jobs, in housing, and in hotels and restaurants. To the Puerto Ricans, who came from a combination of Taino, African, and Spanish backgrounds, this was a new experience. They quickly learned that family members and friends with lighter skin often had better luck finding work and made more money.

Early Puerto Rican migrants also faced racial prejudice from other immigrant groups, especially those from European countries. In the workplace, other immigrants often refused to sit next to or work with their Puerto Rican coworkers. On the streets, Puerto Ricans were often targeted for violence.

Adding to this prejudice was the fact that many migrants needed to receive welfare benefits. This happened because many could not find jobs that paid well enough to support their families. Many people on the mainland accused the Puerto Ricans of migrating solely for the welfare programs. In fact, most Puerto Ricans considered it a terrible disgrace to be on welfare. Puerto Rican men and women took great pride in their work.

The language barrier was another obstacle Puerto Rican migrants faced. Spanish was the official language of the island. English was not used for everyday life. When they moved to the mainland, most of the Spanish–speaking islanders understood little, if any, English.

NATIONALIST MOVEMENT

Puerto Rican nationalists believed that the island should be a free nation. Many nationalists argued that the only way to free Puerto Rico was to wage war on the United States. Protesters rallied both on the island and on the mainland. While many of these nationalist demonstrations were peaceful, some were not.

In 1950 Puerto Rican nationalists attacked the home of U.S. president Harry S. Truman. Truman was not hurt, but the attack forced the Puerto Rican National Guard to round up and arrest many nationalist rebels.

This picture shows a diagrammed view of Blair House, scene of the attempt on President Truman's life by Puerto Rican nationalist rebels.

Kenneth A. Roberts, one of the congressmen wounded in the House of Representatives attack, is carried down the Capitol Building steps on a stretcher.

The most infamous of these attacks, however, occurred on March 1, 1954, when three men and one woman entered the U.S. House of Representatives and shot at the representatives. Five representatives were wounded in the shooting. The shooters were caught and sent to prison to serve life sentences. President Jimmy Carter eventually released the attackers years later.

Not knowing the language created problems. Children struggled with their English-language homework. Adults could not fill out job applications or pass job interviews without English skills. Many employers refused to hire workers who could not speak English. Not knowing English also meant that Puerto Ricans with jobs had very little chance of advancing to higher and better-paying positions.

During the 1950s, there were no programs to help Spanish-speaking migrants learn English. Many Puerto Ricans learned English on the job. Schoolchildren were not allowed to use their native Spanish in the classroom.

MAKING A LIVING

Because many Puerto Ricans knew little English, they found jobs as unskilled laborers in factories or as farmworkers. Some also found work in service industries, taking jobs as cooks and messengers. These jobs provided them with a steady income— something most had never known in Puerto Rico. But they were often the lowest paying and least desirable jobs in the city. Many found themselves working long hours, sometimes seventy or eighty hours a week, for little money. Puerto Ricans who learned English sometimes found better work or advanced to better positions in their industry.

In New York City, Puerto Rican women typically worked in the garment industry. Puerto Rican men in New York found work in factories, hospitals,

The clothing industry attracted many Puerto Rican women. Working long hours, often for pennies per garment, the women labored at the sewing machines side by side.

hotels, restaurants, and laundries. Puerto Ricans living in the East and the Midwest found work in industrial factories, canneries, garment centers, steel mills, and iron foundries. Those employed in the service industries worked as kitchen helpers, bellhops, dishwashers, busboys, and hospital orderlies. Some Puerto Ricans became civil servants (such as mail carriers), and others found careers in the armed forces.

Some Puerto Ricans worked as seasonal farmhands. When Puerto Rico's sugar season ended in June, thousands of Puerto Rican sugar workers signed contracts with employers to work in the farming fields of the northeastern states.

They picked fruits, vegetables, and other crops by hand. Most of these laborers worked long hours and received minimum wage. Still, some of them stayed on the mainland and became permanent residents.

Despite these early obstacles, many Puerto Rican migrants felt happy to move to the mainland. New York was cold and forbidding in many ways, but it was also one of the most exciting cities in the world. Many migrants found steady work that paid better than their jobs on the island. And many newcomers had friends and relatives already living on the mainland, helping them feel more at home.

LEARNING CURVE

Education presented another problem for Puerto Rican migrants. Because U.S. teachers spoke only English, Puerto Rican children often had a difficult time in school. Many teachers expected a child to either learn English immediately or fail completely. Children were rarely allowed to use Spanish in the classroom. Many schools even

CHECK OUT
WWW.INAMERICABOOKS.COM
FOR TIPS ON RESEARCHING
NAMES IN YOUR FAMILY
HISTORY.

changed their students' name to more American-sounding names. For example, Juan became John and Pedro became Pete. Parents rarely challenged the school system, despite these problems. Most parents felt that any education was better than nothing. To them, education seemed to be the only way for their children to find good jobs. Parents valued high grades and often pushed their children to study hard.

The language barrier and discrimination by teachers and classmates remained serious problems for some students, however. Discouraged, many older students dropped out of school and looked for jobs that didn't require much education. If they were unable to find work, many of these youths banded together into gangs. While most Puerto Rican gangs were at first peaceful, they became violent as they began to clash with opposing

Italian and African American gangs. During the 1950s, as the friction between opposing gangs mounted, gang warfare became a serious problem in New York City.

Even when these gangs became involved in violence and bloodshed, they continued to grow in number. Young Puerto Rican American men who felt lost and defeated in their new home gained a sense of unity and toughness by joining these gangs.

And some of these gangs, while infamous for fighting and turf warfare, became important forces in the Puerto Rican American community. The Young Lords, for example, turned their attention to politics. The Young Lords sought to improve educational opportunities for Puerto Rican American students and to make migrants aware that their votes could influence politics in a positive way.

This Young Lords poster calls for a conference of all Puerto Rican students at Columbia University.

LIBERATE PUERTO RICO NOW!

THE
YOUNG
LORDS
PARTY

CALLS FOR
A

CONFERENCE
OF ALL
PUERTO
RICAN
STUDENTS

At Columbia
University
On September
22 and 23
9:00 A.M.

to:

Establish LIBERATE
PUERTO RICO NOW
committees

Mobilize for MASS
DEMONSTRATION
at United Nations
Building on Oct.
30·DAY of JAYUYA

FAMILY MATTERS

Poor jobs and poor housing were not the only problems Puerto Ricans faced on the mainland. Living on the mainland also threatened the structure of many Puerto Rican families. One factor contributing to the breakup of many families was the new social position of

33

Puerto Rican women. In Puerto Rico, most women stayed at home and took care of their children. A husband served as the unquestioned head of the family. On the mainland, however, Puerto Rican women worked outside the home and dealt with teachers, doctors, and others. Many Puerto Rican husbands resented this new independence of their wives. Wives sometimes earned more than their husbands did, something that hurt the pride of many Puerto Rican men. A final humiliation for some men came when their wives found work when they could not. Having their wives support them and their families was more than some Puerto Rican men could accept. Because of these problems, many Puerto Rican migrants found their marriages falling apart.

Other family problems plagued the Puerto Rican migrants. Puerto Rican children enjoyed a new–found freedom on the mainland. Many rebelled against the old–fashioned attitudes of their parents. This was particularly true of Puerto Rican girls. In Puerto Rico, they had been closely guarded and strictly chaperoned. On the mainland, they ventured outside their homes and engaged in a much freer social life than they had ever known before. Puerto Ricans came from a society where children were expected to respect and obey their parents without question. Many Puerto Rican parents found it difficult to accept the relaxed rules followed by children in mainland society.

Another source of friction between parents and children was language. Many children learned

THEY DID NOT REALLY WANT TO BECOME SOMETHING ELSE; THEY DIDN'T WANT TO CHANGE THEIR WAYS OR THEIR LANGUAGE.

—*Victor Hernández Cruz, explaining why his parents wouldn't learn English while living in America*

English much faster than their parents did. Because of this, Puerto Rican youths adapted to American society more quickly than their parents. Young Puerto Ricans abandoned their Puerto Rican customs and heritage to make them seem more American.

Many traditional families (families consisting of a father, mother, and children) fell apart, due to either broken marriages or strained parent–child relations. Extended families, however, remained together on the mainland. Several generations of a family often lived together under the same roof. Family and friends created a sense of community for migrants and their children.

For Puerto Ricans, extended family also included godparents. This is known as *compadrazgo*, or coparenting. Godparents acted as second parents and played an important role in raising their godchildren. Puerto Rican children respected their compadres as they did their parents. In fact, *madrinas*, or "godmothers," often bought the wedding rings for their godchildren when they got engaged. During the holidays, parents gave gifts to the people with whom they had compadrazgo relationships. Compadres also took over the role of raising their godchildren if something happened to their parents.

The compadrazgo concept also helped new migrant families settle into mainland life. A mainland family often formed a compadre relationship with a new migrant family to offer support and advice during the transition.

WALKING THE POVERTY LINE

While many migrants made more money on the mainland than they ever had in Puerto Rico, the high cost of living in New York City kept them in poverty. By the time they paid for food, clothing, transportation, and housing, there was little or no money left over. And as U.S. citizens living on the mainland, they paid state and federal taxes—something they didn't face back in Puerto Rico.

Since most Puerto Ricans found only low-paying jobs, they lived in the poorest neighborhoods. For those in New York, this meant living in the inner-city slums. Puerto Ricans began concentrating in East Harlem, an area on the east side of Manhattan. By the 1950s, so many were living in the area that it became known as Spanish Harlem, or El Barrio, which is Spanish for "the neighborhood." Large numbers of Puerto Ricans settled in other areas of the city, such as the East Bronx, but El Barrio was the area most strongly identified with New York City's Puerto Rican population.

Because New York has such a high cost of living, many immigrants lived in conditions very similar to those in the Puerto Rican slums. In El Barrio, drying laundry hanging over backyards heaped with rubbish was a common sight.

Housing in El Barrio and other Puerto Rican districts in New York City was overcrowded, high priced, and run-down. In many cases, a family of seven or more people lived in a tiny three-room apartment consisting of a living room, which doubled as a bedroom, and a bathroom and kitchen. Less fortunate families lived in a single room, sharing a common bathroom and kitchen with several other families. Whatever the size of the apartment, living conditions were often the same: cracked ceilings and

> *You resign yourself to poverty—my mother did this. . . . You've never seen anything else. Like the only thing we knew was that block. You never went out of that block . . . . I didn't know that there were people who were living much, much better.*
>
> *—writer Felipe Luciano, talking about life in El Barrio*

walls, broken windows, bad plumbing, poor heating, and rats.

Many Puerto Rican families lived below the poverty line. (The poverty line is considered the minimum income necessary to meet a family's basic needs, such as housing and food.) Even with both parents working, most Puerto Rican families could not afford better housing. In fact, many couldn't even afford to live in the slums. As a result, they turned to city, state, and federal agencies for financial aid.

UNITED THEY STAND

Gang fights, lack of education, broken homes, discrimination, unemployment, poor housing, and the language barrier—all of these were serious problems for Puerto Ricans on the mainland. They needed to find ways to solve their problems and to improve the quality of their lives. To do this, they formed several organizations that worked to unite the mainland Puerto Rican community.

One of the most successful groups was the National Puerto Rican Forum (NPRF). New York City Puerto Ricans established the NPRF during the mid–1950s. The NPRF was organized to give the Puerto Ricans of New York City a voice. The forum brought the migrants together as a unified group. Under this organization, New York City's Puerto Rican community attacked its problems and worked for improvements with greater power and strength than ever before. Other organizations provided assistance to the Puerto Rican community through counseling, job-training

The Liga Puertorriqueña was formed in 1922 to unite the various Puerto Rican clubs and organizations in New York. Like other clubs that followed it, the Liga promoted unity and social and cultural activities.

programs, youth organizations, and housing projects. The Puerto Rican Family Institute was instrumental in helping Puerto Rican migrants adjust to life on the mainland. The Puerto Rican Association for Community Affairs operated day-care centers, health clinics, bilingual and bicultural educational programs, and other support services for the Puerto Rican community. Groups such as the Puerto Rican Merchants Association helped small Puerto Rican businesses and business owners. And groups such as the Puerto Rican Forum tried to help troubled Puerto Rican youths.

To promote cultural awareness and pride, the Institute of Puerto Rican Culture was founded in New York City in 1955. To further promote Puerto Rican pride, New York City Puerto Ricans started the National

PUERTO RICANS SYMBOLICALLY MAKE THEIR CLAIM TO THE CITY AS A WHOLE AS THEY MARCH ALONG MANHATTAN'S FIFTH AVENUE THROUGH NON-PUERTO RICAN NEIGHBORHOODS. THE . . . MESSAGE IS: "NEW YORK IS OURS TOO."

—Writer Vicky Muñiz, commenting on the National Puerto Rican Day Parade

Puerto Rican Day Parade in 1958. The parade, which takes place every year on the second Sunday in June, celebrates the contributions and accomplishments of New York's Puerto Rican community.

Despite these advances, Puerto Rican migrants still needed to deal with the two most serious issues that they faced—the language barrier and unequal education opportunities. In 1961 Puerto Rican leaders established the organization ASPIRA. The organization worked to keep Puerto Rican students in school and challenged them to learn. ASPIRA offered courses, including English lessons, to young and old alike. ASPIRA encouraged school-age Puerto Ricans to finish high school and go onto college. ASPIRA also offered job-training programs, scholarship funds, English-tutoring programs, and youth clubs in junior and senior high schools throughout the nation. In addition, ASPIRA helped break through the language barriers.

Many of the organizations that were formed in the twentieth century worked to promote a positive image of Puerto Ricans in New York City, such as this photographic exhibit on Puerto Rican culture held at the New York Public Library in 1947. For more information on modern Puerto Rican organizations, go to www.inamericabooks.com for links.

3

MAKING THEIR MARK

Life for the Puerto Ricans living in New York and other mainland cities was not easy, but it was not all bad either. Many jobs were low paying and undesirable, but at least they were jobs. The tenements (housing with poor living conditions) were old and dingy, but they were better than no homes at all. The cities were cold and forbidding, but friends and family were always there to give warmth and comfort. If life on the mainland was not the best of all possible worlds, neither was it the worst. And despite the many problems, mainland Puerto Ricans had managed to create their own unique community. New York City's El Barrio became the most important and most famous of these communities.

web enhanced at **www.inamericabooks.com**

El Barrio

Movie houses showing Spanish-language films, travel agencies offering low-cost flights back to Puerto Rico, and candy stores featuring jukeboxes that played Spanish-language records all marked the streets of El Barrio. The neighborhood featured restaurants and bakeries, laundries and clothing shops, dance halls and bars, and *bodegas*—small grocery stores selling fruits, vegetables, and foods imported from Puerto Rico.

Storefront churches stood among the many stores of the tightly packed neighborhood. These churches consisted of small, tightly knit congregations and featured lively services with plenty of singing and clapping. Most important, the churches served a social function by sponsoring recreation centers, athletic clubs, and other activities.

FIND LINKS TO LOCATE PUERTO RICAN EVENTS AND ACTIVITIES IN YOUR AREA AT WWW.INAMERICABOOKS.COM.

During New York's long, cold winter, El Barrio's streets were nearly deserted. Most Puerto Ricans stayed indoors, venturing out into the forbidding cold only for work, school, and shopping. But when summer arrived, the streets of El Barrio hummed with activity. Radios and bands filled the air with Latin music, and people gathered in front of their houses for informal meetings and sidewalk parties. While children played stickball and other street games, teenagers and young adults went to dance halls for dance contests and to listen to local bands.

BODEGAS

A bodega is a small grocery store that specializes in Latin American products. Bodegas in New York City cater to Puerto Ricans, selling food and other items from the island that American grocers do not. Spanish-language newspapers are also sold at these small shops.

But bodegas are an important part of their communities. They serve as meeting places for friends. Many bodega owners even extend a line of credit to their regular customers so they can buy items during the week and then pay their bill when they receive their paycheck.

Puerto Ricans shop at La Marqueta, a five-block-long Spanish marketplace in New York City. Such bodegas are sprinkled throughout the city, offering people tastes of home and an opportunity to mingle with fellow migrants.

Colorful and exciting, El Barrio was one of the friendliest and most tightly knit communities. The Puerto Ricans formed warm, lasting friendships in El Barrio. They usually shared what little they had with their friends and neighbors. No matter how poor they were, the Puerto Ricans never failed to open their doors and their hearts to hungry children and adults.

This warmth and affection was most evident within Puerto Rican families. Puerto Ricans in El Barrio and other Puerto Rican districts on the mainland frequently lived with, or very close to, their relatives. In many cases, they served as godparents to their brothers' and sisters' children.

IDENTITY CRISIS

Perhaps the most serious problem that mainland Puerto Ricans faced, however, was that of identity. Since many of the Puerto Ricans living on the mainland still looked upon Puerto Rico as their *real* home, they felt as if they did not really belong to the mainland. This feeling of not belonging was strengthened by the fact that thousands of Puerto Ricans on the mainland returned home to Puerto Rico each year. And Puerto Ricans born on the mainland sometimes felt caught between cultures. While they were members of both the island and the mainland, both lands considered them foreigners.

> *As Puerto Ricans, we grew up with contradictions and in contradictions. Are we Americans? Well, not really. Are we Puerto Rican? Well, we may never have been to Puerto Rico. . . . There are parts of here that are us and parts of there that are not us. So we grow up with . . . a sense of belonging to neither place.*
>
> —*Political activist Blanca Vasquez*

This identity crisis for Puerto Ricans was also linked with the reluctance of the migrants to get involved in mainland politics. Since the first Puerto Rican Americans did not see themselves as permanent residents of the mainland, they did not feel it was important to establish many political organizations. As U.S. citizens living on the mainland, the Puerto Ricans had every right to participate in political activities and to vote in political elections. But since many of the first–generation migrants believed they would someday return to Puerto Rico, they did not register to vote or engage in politics. As a result, they had no representatives in the city, state, and federal governments to fight for them or to help improve the quality of their lives on the mainland.

In politics, language again presented a problem. Before 1965, citizens living in New York and several other mainland cities were required to take a literacy test in English before registering to vote. Since many early Puerto Rican migrants couldn't read English, they failed the test and were denied the right to vote. Without a voice in government, mainland Puerto Ricans could do little to improve their social condition.

NUYORICANS

Most young Puerto Ricans living on the mainland considered themselves both Puerto Rican and American. These children of the early migrants were rooted in both island and mainland life, and they accepted both cultures as their own. Instead of blending into mainstream American life, young Puerto Ricans strove to integrate Puerto Rican traditions and heritage with their American way of life. This created an entirely new identity for the children of the early Puerto Rican migrants.

Second–generation Puerto Ricans born in New York City are called Nuyoricans, a combination of New York and Puerto Rican. While the original term reflected the early migrants' close association with New York City, the meaning has changed to include anyone raised in America whose parents are Puerto Rican. Unlike their parents, many Nuyoricans considered America their permanent home. When their families returned to the island, Nuyoricans often found themselves homesick for their U.S. cities. In addition, English–speaking Nuyoricans found themselves facing discrimination and rejection from the Spanish–speaking islanders.

Because they had one foot in each culture, they often felt foreign in both. Many young Nuyoricans worked to develop their own, unique identity that combined the best of both worlds. To bolster this new identity and pride, the Nuyorican Poets Café opened in the 1960s. The café allowed Nuyorican writers and artists to share their works in an understanding environment. As Nuyorican pride grew, more young people began embracing their Puerto Rican heritage. Musical styles from the island, such as the *bomba* and the salsa, enjoyed a new popularity among young Puerto Ricans living in the mainland United States. Bomba music has its roots in African rhythms and features a singer and drums. The words are usually improvised, meaning that musicians make up the words as they go, but they usually revolve around community events. Also essential to bomba are dancers.

The Nuyorican Poets Café celebrates and promotes the unique role Puerto Rican heritage plays in New York City culture.

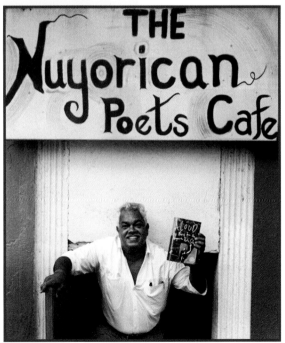

Salsa music combines fast-tempo African and Caribbean rhythms with big band jazz. A typical salsa band often includes singers, trumpets and saxophones, a bass, and a strong percussion section.

Another example of Nuyoricans combining their heritage and their new home is in their cuisine. Many Puerto Rican Americans, especially younger generations, eat American fare. Favorite foods often include pizza, fast food, and hot dogs. While many mainland families have adopted these foods, they have also kept their more traditional recipes— especially for holidays and special occasions. Common herbs, flavorings, and seasonings are cilantro, lime, and *sofrito* (a sauce made from onion, green pepper, and garlic). Desserts include tropical fruits and a rich custard known as flan.

Nuyoricans also developed their own language. Most Nuyoricans were bilingual—they spoke both Spanish, the language of the island, and English, the language of the mainland. Most second- and third-generation Puerto Rican migrants used English for their jobs and in schools, but they spoke Spanish at home.

Many Nuyoricans began using a combination of both languages in their everyday speech. This combination language became known as Spanglish. It also used both languages in the same sentence, and it adapted English words to sound more Spanish. For example, the word *elevador* meant "elevator," and *yarda* became Spanglish for "yard."

COCONUT FLAN

Flan is a rich custard dessert. Puerto Rican chefs like to use a variety of tropical fruits to flavor their flan, sometimes using pineapple or mango, but coconut flan remains one of the most popular versions of this tasty treat. To learn how to prepare other Puerto Rican dishes, visit www.inamericabooks.com for links.

1 C. GRANULATED SUGAR

6 EGGS

12-OZ. CAN EVAPORATED MILK

14-OZ. CAN COCONUT MILK

14-OZ. CAN SWEETENED
    CONDENSED MILK

1 TBSP. VANILLA EXTRACT

1. Preheat oven to 350°F.
2. Caramelize the sugar by pouring it into a small saucepan and placing over low heat. Cook for 8 to 10 minutes or until melted, stirring constantly so that it doesn't burn. When sugar begins to bubble, remove saucepan from heat. Carefully and quickly pour caramelized sugar into a 9 × 9-inch baking pan. Cool.
3. Beat eggs lightly and add remaining ingredients. Beat until well blended.
4. Pour mixture through a strainer into the baking pan.
5. Fill a large pan with enough hot water to come about halfway up the side of the baking pan. Place in oven and bake 45 to 50 minutes, or until toothpick inserted in center comes out clean.
6. Remove from oven and allow flan to cool on a rack. To serve, dip the flan pan briefly in warm water and invert pan onto a serving platter.

Serves 8 to 10

Mainland Puerto Rican literature soon embraced this bilingualism. Writers began using Spanish, English, or even Spanglish for their works. These works started focusing on the obstacles Puerto Rican migrants faced in the struggle to find their identity as both Puerto Ricans and Americans.

A Growing Voice

During the 1960s, more than one million Puerto Ricans lived on the mainland, most in New York City. But they remained largely invisible to U.S. society. They generally worked behind the scenes, washing dishes in restaurants, cleaning hotels and hospitals, or working on factory lines. Few regarded Puerto Ricans as "real" Americans, despite their citizenship.

The mainland Puerto Rican population continued to grow in the late 1960s. At the same time, minority groups in America, particularly African Americans, began demanding equal rights. Many Latino groups, including the Puerto Ricans, joined this push to end discrimination and unfair treatment. Community leaders worked to improve the most pressing

I am not African. Africa is in me, but I cannot return. I am not Taina. Taino is in me, but there is no way back. I am not European. Europe lives in me, but I have no home there. I am new. History made me. My first language was Spanglish. I was born at the crossroads and I am whole.

—Poet Aurora Levins Morales

issues that the Puerto Rican population faced.

As a result, new programs sprang up to help the large Spanish-speaking communities. New York City libraries, for example, began reaching out to Spanish-speaking peoples. They offered bilingual assistants and started programs to bring Puerto Rican culture to their readers. Puerto Rican cultural forums also grew from this drive for equality.

FIND LINKS FOR MORE INFORMATION ABOUT THE MANY WAYS THAT PEOPLE OF PUERTO RICAN HERITAGE CONTRIBUTE TO LIFE IN AMERICA AT WWW.INAMERICABOOKS.COM.

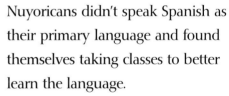

El Museo del Barrio, the Museum of the Barrio, opened its doors in 1969. The museum featured works by Puerto Rican and other Latino artists. The Puerto Rican Traveling Theater was also founded to support talented Puerto Rican artists, both actors and playwrights.

The Nuyorican influence began stretching all the way back to Puerto Rico as Nuyoricans visited, or sometimes even settled on, the island. They brought their mainland way of life with them. For example, the town of Levittown, Puerto Rico, developed an atmosphere similar to New York. Levittown started looking more like a mainland city as the same stores and restaurants sprang up. And many people living in Levittown started speaking English as their main language. Some Nuyoricans didn't speak Spanish as their primary language and found themselves taking classes to better learn the language.

By 1970 nearly 1.4 million Puerto Ricans lived in the mainland United States. At that time, more Puerto Ricans lived in New York City than in San Juan, the capital of Puerto Rico. Puerto Ricans living on the mainland had worked hard to build a sense of self and a sense of community. While many considered the mainland their permanent home, the island remained an important part of their heritage and identity.

Levittown, Puerto Rico, is in many ways indistinguishable from New York City. Nuyoricans have brought their mainland lifestyle to the island, including American restaurants, shops, and clothing.

MAKING CHANGES

Puerto Rico's economy suffered in the 1970s due to rising oil prices and a loss of foreign investment. More migrants traveled to the mainland. This new wave differed from earlier migrations, however. Many Puerto Ricans who relocated to the mainland possessed college degrees from Puerto Rican universities and had worked as professionals on the island. But some of the poorest Puerto Ricans moved to the mainland as well. At the same time, many first-generation migrants began retiring to the island.

All of these factors created two very different social classes of mainland Puerto Rican migrants. This in turn presented new problems for the question of migrant identity. Many of these Puerto Rican professionals settled far from Puerto Rican neighborhoods, for example. And they often blended more easily into the American way of life than their poorer counterparts. This gave them less reason to connect with the organizations working to help other Puerto Rican migrants.

Despite this split between the groups, community leaders focused on winning the rights that Puerto Ricans should have had as U.S. citizens, such as the right to join unions and the right to better government services. Many civil rights groups organized during the 1970s and early 1980s. Among these were the Coalition in Defense of Puerto Rican and Hispanic Rights and the National Congress for Puerto Rican Rights. These groups worked to represent migrants' interests and to protect their rights.

Puerto Ricans had become the second-largest Spanish-speaking population in the mainland United States by the 1980s, with the largest group being Mexicans. As their numbers grew, so did their voice. Puerto Rican community leaders wanted to encourage people to become more active in politics. This would give them more representation in the government. In 1987 the Office of the Commonwealth promoted a voter-registration drive called *Atrevete*, "I dare you to register." The project encouraged Puerto Rican Americans to get involved in the American political system by voting. By 1992 these programs had made a difference. Puerto Rican voters in Chicago elected Luis Gutierrez to the House of Representatives (House). And New York voters elected Nydia Velazquez to the House in 1992, making her the first Puerto Rican woman to serve in the U.S. Congress (Puerto Rican members of the House only vote in committees).

Puerto Rican migrants who moved to the mainland during the 1990s and the early part of the new millennium made more changes from earlier migrants.

STATUS QUO

Puerto Rico's political status remains a hot issue for both islanders and mainland Puerto Ricans. The country may choose to remain a commonwealth. This means Puerto Rico stays under U.S. control, but its people cannot vote for the U.S. president. Its second choice is statehood. This would make the island part of the United States, giving it the full rights of any U.S. state. The third choice is to become an independent nation. As a nation, Puerto Ricans would elect their own president but might lose some of the trade advantages it has as a U.S. commonwealth. Many mainlanders argue for statehood, and many islanders believe commonwealth status or independence would be best. In 1998 Puerto Ricans voted to remain a commonwealth. While the island's future status remains unclear, it is clear that Puerto Ricans feel passionately about their homeland.

In 1998 Congresswoman Nydia Velazquez became the first Hispanic woman to serve as chair or ranking member of a full committee in the history of the House of Representatives.

First, many did not head directly for New York City. Instead, they found work and homes in other large cities, such as Chicago, Los Angeles, and Philadelphia. While New York remains the center of the mainland Puerto Rican population, the percentage of Puerto Ricans living in the city in the 1990s had dropped nearly 30 percent since the 1950s.

Another important change for mainland Puerto Rican communities was the education system. In the early 2000s, many more Puerto Rican migrants graduated from high school and went on to college or technical schools than in the 1990s. Increased education opened more doors for them in the workplace. Puerto Ricans began filling more and more skilled and professional positions. This in turn meant that Puerto Rican workers earned better wages. By 1993 about 50 percent of Puerto Rican American workers held professional or technical jobs. Many Nuyoricans work as lawyers, doctors, teachers, and social workers. Some own their own businesses, including restaurants, grocery stores, newspapers, laundries, banks, barbershops, and small factories. In turn, many of these professionals continue to work to develop organizations that improve the Puerto Rican community.

Since Nuyoricans often speak English as their primary language, some needed to take Spanish lessons to help them communicate with relatives and friends living on the island. While Nuyoricans

FIND LINKS TO READ
THE LATEST PUERTO
RICAN NEWS AT
WWW.INAMERICABOOKS.COM.

wanted to maintain their Puerto Rican heritage, they also wanted to develop their identities as U.S. citizens.

By the early 2000s, statistics show that the estimated number of Puerto Ricans living on the mainland will outnumber the number living in Puerto Rico. Most of the new wave of migrants are highly educated professionals who are unable to find work on the island. In addition, the new Puerto Rican migrants recognize the importance of being politically active. Each year, more and more Puerto Rican Americans register to vote. This helps them pass new laws and win new programs that benefit the Puerto Rican community. Through their political activities, they are also able to improve housing conditions and employment and education opportunities.

Another way Puerto Ricans have worked to improve their life in America is through community

A group of Puerto Ricans in New York City show their support for Hillary Rodham Clinton, who was a guest of honor at the 2000 National Puerto Rican Day Parade.

cleanups. Organizers in New York City clean up empty lots, erect small houses, and plant gardens there. These lots, known as *casitas*, become small cultural centers for the community. Musicians perform various types of Puerto Rican music, such as the *plena* and the salsa. Plenas warn people about the dangers of drugs and crime. Salsa musicians help promote pride in the Puerto Rican culture.

Proud of their rich heritage, thousands of Puerto Ricans waving Puerto Rican flags line the parade route during the National Puerto Rican Day Parade in New York City.

FORGING AHEAD

Despite political unity and cultural pride, Puerto Ricans living on the mainland still face some of the same hardships that earlier generations faced. Some Puerto Rican families still live below the poverty line. And Puerto Ricans remain the poorest of all the

Hispanic groups in the mainland United States. Some poorer Puerto Rican youths do not attend school, making it harder to find jobs and break out of this cycle. Racism, while no longer as socially accepted as it was when the first Puerto Rican migrants settled on the mainland, still affects some Puerto Ricans. This remains especially true for those migrants who do not speak English.

Some Puerto Ricans still consider their life in the mainland United States as temporary. It is a way to provide their family with a good education and to make more money than they would on the island. For these migrants, adapting to their new culture while retaining ties with their old way of life presents the same identity problems that earlier migrants faced.

Family remains an important institution for mainland Puerto Ricans. But the structure of mainland families has changed. About half of the Puerto Rican families living in New York City in the late 1990s were headed by single women. Still other families combine children and parents from previous marriages, bringing half-brothers and half-sisters into the mix. Extended family includes relatives and friends living on the island. Phone calls and visits help mainland Puerto Ricans stay in touch with their loved ones as well as their roots.

The growing migrant population has also led to a

[Being Puerto Rican is] like a child jumping double dutch . . . two ropes [Puerto Rican and American identity] going in opposite directions very quickly. . . . It is a constant juggling, a constant jumping up and down trying to be in one place or another.

—Esmeralda Santiago, author of When I Was Puerto Rican

55

crossover to mainstream culture. Puerto Rican and Latino music and literature enjoy a wide following outside of the Puerto Rican community. Many Nuyorican writers appeal to a wider American audience. These writers include Piri Thomas, author of *Down These Mean Streets*, whose works paint a picture of Puerto Rican life on the mainland. Musical forms such as the salsa have also crossed over to mainstream America with musicians such as Tito Puente. Puerto Rican painters and sculptors use their

Artist Paul Santaleri painted this mural at Fifth and Olive Streets in Philadelphia. It is called Through Cracks in the Pavement *and symbolizes hope and possibility through its portrayal of things that grow up through concrete.*

art as political or social messages, which are displayed in many U.S. museums. Puerto Rican murals appear throughout the United States, mainly in New York, Chicago, and Philadelphia. Puerto Rican entertainers are also coming to the forefront of mainland cinema as more Nuyorican and Puerto Rican American actors and actresses such as Jennifer Lopez gain celebrity.

Thousands of Puerto Ricans continue to arrive on the mainland each year. But at the same time, thousands of Puerto Ricans living on the mainland return to the

island. Thus the current migration of Puerto Ricans to the mainland is very small. As Puerto Rican families on the mainland (especially in cities such as New York and Chicago) continue to grow in size, however, Puerto Rican Americans continue to be an increasingly visible and influential population in the mainland United States. Creating an identity as both Puerto Ricans and as Americans is an important bridge between their past and their future.

VIEQUES

Probably the most important hot-button political topic for most Puerto Rican Americans is the island of Vieques. For more than sixty years, the island was used as a training base and for war games by the U.S. Navy. Most Puerto Ricans, both islanders and mainlanders, protested these military practices—including bombing campaigns—fearing for the rare plants and animals that inhabit the island. On May 1, 2003, after years of public protests on the mainland and the island, the U.S. Navy pulled out of Vieques. The U.S. government transferred Vieques's fate to the Department of the Interior, an agency that has promised to clean up the island and convert it into the largest wildlife refuge in the Caribbean. Puerto Rican Americans, who understand the power of their growing political voice, will likely pay close attention to these cleanup efforts.

FAMOUS PUERTO RICAN AMERICANS

HERMAN BADILLO (b. 1929)

Born in Caguas, Puerto Rico, Herman Badillo is a politician who became the first Puerto Rican to win a seat (non–voting) in the U.S. House of Representatives. Badillo moved to New York in 1941, where he put himself through college and law school. After graduating he entered politics, and in 1970 he was elected to the U.S. Congress. In 1983 he became chair of the Governor's Advisory Committee on Hispanic Affairs.

ROBERTO CLEMENTE (1934–1972)

Born in Carolina, Puerto Rico, Roberto Clemente played professional baseball on the island until he moved to the U.S. mainland to join the Pittsburgh

Pirates as an outfielder. During his seventeen–year career with the Pirates, he won many awards, including Most Valuable Player of

the World Series in 1971. In 1972, just a few months after his death in a plane crash, he was elected to the Baseball Hall of Fame.

BENICIO DEL TORO (b. 1967)

Benicio del Toro is an actor who was born in San German, Puerto Rico. Del Toro studied acting in New York and worked in theater until he caught the eye of several film directors. Unlike earlier Latino actors, del Toro has had the opportunity to break away from stereotypical roles and to portray a variety of complex characters. His movies include *The Usual Suspects*, *Basquiat*, *Fear and Loathing in Las Vegas*, and *21 Grams*. In 2001 he won an Academy Award for his performance in the movie *Traffic*.

ORLANDO FIGUEROA (b. 1955)

Orlando Figueroa was born in San Juan, Puerto Rico, and earned a college degree in mechanical engineering from the University of

Puerto Rico. He moved to the mainland United States to study at the University of Maryland. In 2001 NASA appointed Figueroa as director of its Mars Exploration Program in the Office of Space Science. In this position, he is in charge of directing the robotic exploration of the planet Mars.

JENNIFER LOPEZ (b. 1970)

Jennifer Lopez, an actress and singer of Puerto Rican descent, was born in

the Bronx in New York City. Lopez started her career singing and dancing in musicals. She performed with The Fly Girls on the television show *In Living Color*. Soon after, she made her film debut in the movie *Mi Familia*. But real fame came with the title role in the movie *Selena*. Her movie credits also include *U-Turn, Out of Sight, The Wedding Planner,* and *Maid in Manhattan*. Lopez is also a popular singer, and her album "On the Six" reached platinum.

RICKY MARTIN (b. 1971)

Born in San Juan, Puerto Rico, Ricky Martin started his career with Menudo, a

Puerto Rican singing group that gained popularity in the United States in the early 1980s. Menudo recorded albums in both Spanish and English and toured throughout the United States. In 1998 Martin achieved solo stardom with his hit "Living la Vida Loca." His music is a blend of rock, pop, and salsa. Martin lives in Miami, Florida.

RITA MORENO (b. 1931)

Rita Moreno is an actress and dancer who was born in Hurnacao, Puerto Rico. When she was six years old, she moved to New York with her mother. At seventeen Moreno starred in

her first Broadway play. She is listed in the *Guinness Book of World Records* as the only performer ever to win all four of the entertainment industry's most prestigious awards: the Oscar (1962), the Grammy (1972), the Tony (1975), and the Emmy (1977 and 1978). She is perhaps best known for her role as Anita in *West Side Story*, for which she won an Oscar.

ANTONIA NOVELLO (b. 1944)
Antonia Novello served as U.S. surgeon general from 1990 to 1993. Novello, who was born in Fajardo, Puerto Rico, received her medical degree from the University of Puerto Rico in 1970. She moved to the mainland and earned a master's degree in public health from Johns Hopkins University in 1982. As surgeon general, she focused on publicizing the dangers of smoking, expanding AIDS education, and improving health care for women and children. In 1993 Novello went to work for the United Nations Children's Fund (UNICEF).

ROSIE PEREZ (b. 1964) Rosie Perez is an actress of Puerto Rican  descent who was born in Brooklyn, a borough of New York City. While going to college in Los Angeles, Perez was discovered by movie director Spike Lee. She starred in Lee's movie *Do the Right Thing*. Since then she has appeared in a number of successful films, including *White Men Can't Jump*, *Night on Earth*, and *Untamed Heart*. She was also a choreographer and dancer on the television comedy show *In Living Color*.

TITO PUENTE (1923–2000) Tito Puente, known as the Mambo King, was a musician credited with developing the music known as salsa. Puente grew up in New York  City, the son of Puerto Rican migrants. He attended Juilliard School of Music to study composing and conducting. A multitalented musician, Puente played saxophone, conga drums, bongos, and vibraphones. He performed with his band, the Picadilly Boys, playing mambo, jazz, pop, and cha–cha music.

ABRAHAM RODRIGUEZ JR. (b. 1961) Born in the Bronx in New York City, Abraham Rodriguez Jr. is an important Puerto Rican American author who has achieved national recognition. Raised in the Bronx, Rodriguez began writing when he was very young. His novels portray life growing up in the South Bronx. His books *Boy without a Flag* and

Spidertown provide an important voice for modern young Puerto Rican Americans struggling with poverty in their inner-city neighborhoods. His newest book is titled *The Buddha Book*.

JUAN "CHI CHI" RODRIGUEZ (b. 1935) Chi Chi

Rodriguez, born in Bayamón, Puerto Rico, was a golf caddie who became a professional golfer in 1960. Four years later, Rodriguez was one of the leading tournament winners of the Professional Golf Association. He has represented Puerto Rico in the World Cup Tournament in Singapore. He graduated to the PGA Senior Tour in 1985.

JESÚS MARÍA SANROMÁ

(1902–1984) Jesús María Sanromá was

a concert pianist born in Carolina, Puerto Rico. After moving to the U.S. mainland in 1917, he studied piano at the New England Conservatory of Music. From 1926 to 1943, he was the official pianist of the Boston Symphony. Sanromá gave recitals in London, Paris, Vienna, Madrid, and scores of U.S. cities.

ESMERALDA SANTIAGO (b. 1928)

Esmeralda Santiago was born in San Juan, Puerto Rico. She moved to the mainland United States with her family at the age of thirteen. She graduated *magna cum laude* from Harvard in 1976 and started a film and media production company with her husband. She has also written several memoirs, a novel, and is coeditor of several anthologies. Her memoir *Almost a Woman* was adapted for film by ExxonMobil Masterpiece Theatre in 2002.

PIRI THOMAS (b. 1928) Born in

New York City, Piri Thomas is a Puerto Rican American writer whose most important work is *Down These Mean Streets*, an autobiographical novel published in 1967. The best-selling book tells the story of Thomas's life in the ghettos of East Harlem. *Down These Mean Streets* was such a success that in 1968, the book was made into an award-winning documentary entitled *The World of Piri Thomas*.

TIMELINE

ca. A.D. 1000	The Taino first arrive on the island they call Boriquén.
1493	Columbus claims Boriquén for Spain.
1508	Ponce de León explores the island.
1509	The first Spanish settlement is established on the island.
1523	The island's first sugarcane processing plant opens.
1786	The first history of the island is published, *Historia Geográfica, Civil y Política de Puerto Rico* (*Geographic, Civil and Political History of Puerto Rico*).
1815	The Spanish king opens Puerto Rico to trade from other nations.
1868	Ramón Emeterio Betances leads a small uprising and declares Puerto Rico's independence from Spain. The revolt is quickly put down.
1897	Spain grants Puerto Rico partial self-rule.
1898	The Treaty of Paris makes Puerto Rico a U.S. possession.
1900	The Foraker Act establishes a Puerto Rican civilian government.
1917	The Jones Act gives Puerto Ricans limited U.S. citizenship.
1948	The Office of the Commonwealth opens in New York City.
1951	Puerto Ricans draft their first constitution.
1952	The United States recognizes Puerto Rico as a self-governing commonwealth.

1953	The largest migration of Puerto Ricans to the mainland occurs.
1954	Puerto Rican nationalists open fire in the U.S. House of Representatives.
1955	The Institute of Puerto Rican Culture is founded in New York City.
1958	The first annual National Puerto Rican Day Parade takes place in New York City
1969	El Museo del Barrio opens in New York City.
1987	The Atrevete project encourages Puerto Ricans on the mainland to register to vote.
1992	Nydia Velazquez becomes the first Puerto Rican woman elected to the U.S. Congress.
2000	More than 3.4 million Puerto Ricans live on the U.S. mainland.
2003	The U.S. Navy pulls out of the island of Vieques. The U.S. government designates the area as a wildlife refuge.
2004	For the first time since migration began, more Puerto Ricans live on the mainland than on the island.

GLOSSARY

BILINGUAL: able to speak two languages with equal fluency

COLONY: a territory ruled by another country, usually from some distance away

COMMONWEALTH: a territory that governs its own local affairs but that is also tied to a larger nation through common laws and rights

COMPADRAZGO: Spanish for "coparenting"; the relationship between family friends, similar to that of godparents

IMMIGRATE: to move to live in a country other than one's homeland. A person who immigrates is called an immigrant.

MIGRANT: a person who moves regularly within his or her own country, usually in search of work

NATIONALIST: a person who feels loyalty toward the nation and places a primary emphasis on promoting national culture and national interests

NUYORICANS: second-generation Puerto Rican migrants who were born on the U.S. mainland

PLANTATION: a large estate on which crops are grown, usually with the help of peasant farmers or slave labor

PLENA: a Puerto Rican musical style, usually improvised, that is played on drums

THINGS TO SEE AND DO

EL BORICUA, A BILINGUAL, CULTURAL PUBLICATION FOR PUERTO RICANS
<http://www.elboricua.com/Directory.html>
Check out this directory on the El Boricua website to find Puerto Rican organizations and events in your area.

EL MUSEO DEL BARRIO, NEW YORK, NEW YORK
<http://elmuseo.org>
This museum is dedicated to Puerto Rican, Caribbean, and Latin American art. Literature at the museum is in both Spanish and English.

NATIONAL PUERTO RICAN DAY PARADE, NEW YORK, NEW YORK
<http://nationalpuertoricanday
parade.org/>
The parade, which first occurred in 1958, celebrates the achievements and contributions of New York's Puerto Rican population. Floats, singing, and dancing are all part of the fun. The parade takes place the second Sunday in June.

NEW YORK SALSA FESTIVAL
<http://www.justsalsa.com/>
Started in September 1975, this annual music festival features performances by world-famous Latin American musicians. The festival celebrates and promotes Puerto Rican music and culture. This site offers more information about the festival and about salsa music.

PREGONES THEATER, NEW YORK, NEW YORK
<http://www.pregones.org/Eng/
tickets/viudas_alegres.html>
This organization is dedicated to producing live theater and music rooted in Puerto Rican heritage. The theater's musicals are performed in Spanish, English, or both. The theater's national touring company has appeared in more than three hundred cities.

SEGUNDO RUIZ BELVIS CULTURAL CENTER, CHICAGO, ILLINOIS
<http://www.ruizbelvis.org/>
Founded in 1971, this center seeks to promote pride among Puerto Rican youths and their communities through various artistic and educational programs. The center offers workshops, exhibitions, and activities for youths to demonstrate and share their artistic and musical skills.

SOURCE NOTES

10 Frank de Varona, *Latino Literacy: The Complete Guide to Our Hispanic History and Culture* (New York: Henry Holt and Company, 1996), 128.

18 Stephen Lewin, ed., *The Latino Experience in U.S. History* (Paramus, NJ: Globe Fearon, 1994), 184.

21 Martin Schwabacher, *Puerto Rico* (New York: Marshall Cavendish, 2001), 8.

27 Carmen Dolores Hernandez, *Puerto Rican Voices in English: Interviews with Writers* (Westport, CT: Praeger Publishers, 1997) 176.

34 Ibid, 67.

37 Suzanne Oboler, *Ethnic Labels, Latino Lives: Identity and the Politics of (Re)Presentation in the United States* (Minneapolis: University of Minnesota Press, 1995), 52.

38 Vicky Muñiz, *Resisting Gentrification and Displacement: Voices of Puerto Rican Women of the Barrio* (New York: Garland Publishing, 1998), 144.

43 Ibid, 58.

48 Schwabacher, 9.

55 Juan Flores, *From Bomba to Hip-Hop: Puerto Rican Culture and Latino Identity* (New York: Columbia University Press, 2000), 122.

SELECTED BIBLIOGRAPHY

Davis, Lucile. *Puerto Rico.* New York: Children's Press, 2000. This book covers the history of the island and its people, including a section about Puerto Ricans in America.

De Varona, Frank. *Latino Literacy: The Complete Guide to Our Hispanic History and Culture.* New York: Henry Holt and Company, 1996. This book covers the history and culture of Hispanic Americans, including Puerto Ricans. Special features include a section focusing on Hispanic contributions to the arts and minibiographies of famous Hispanics.

Encyclopaedia Britannica online. N.d. <http://www.britannica.com/eb/article?eu=127867> (February 25, 2004). Encyclopaedia Britannica gives a complete description of the history, geography, and people of Puerto Rico, including a brief discussion of Puerto Rican migrants.

Flores, Juan. *From Bomba to Hip-Hop: Puerto Rican Culture and Latino Identity.* New York: Columbia University Press, 2000. These essays look at Puerto Rican culture and identity on the island and the mainland United States.

Gonzalez, Juan. *Harvest of Empire: A History of Latinos in America.* New York: Viking, 2000. Gonzalez traces the obstacles and achievements of Hispanic groups living in America, including Puerto Ricans.

Himilce, Novas. *Everything You Need to Know about Latino History.* New York: Penguin Putnam Inc., 1998. The section on Puerto Rico answers questions about the culture and history of Puerto Rican migrants.

Lewin, Stephen, ed. *The Latino Experience in U.S. History.* Paramus, NJ: Globe Fearon, 1994. This book looks at the history of Latin American migrants living in the United States, including Puerto Ricans.

Oboler, Suzanne. *Ethnic Labels, Latino Lives: Identity and the Politics of (Re)Presentation in the United States.* Minneapolis: University of Minnesota Press, 1995. This book explores the history of Latin American people in the United States.

Puerto Rico-Boriken. January 12, 2004. <http://www.prboriken.com/> (February 25, 2004). This website gives detailed information about the island and its culture. It also provides links to sites covering Puerto Rican culture, sports, and government.

Shorris, Earl. *Latinos: A Biography of the People.* New York: W. W. Norton & Company, 1992. Shorris looks at the Latino experience in the United States—from language and education obstacles to cultural contributions to American life.

Welcome to Puerto Rico. January 20, 2004. <http://welcome.topuertorico.org> (February 25, 2004). This site covers the Puerto Rican people and culture and gives tourist information about the island.

FURTHER READING & WEBSITES

FICTION

Ada, Alma Flor. *My Name Is Maria Isabel*. New York: Atheneum, 1993. Puerto Rican-born Maria Isabel hopes to fit in at her new school on the mainland.

Cofer, Judith Ortiz. *An Island Like You: Stories of the Barrio*. New York: Orchard Books, 1995. Cofer's twelve fiction stories cover the lives of young people as they struggle between their Puerto Rican heritage in mainland surroundings.

Holohan, Maureen. *Left Out by Rosie*. Wilmette, IL: Broadway Ballplayers, 1998. Eleven-year-old Rosie is a star baseball player and the only girl on her team. But Rosie fears this will never be enough to make her father proud.

Mohr, Nicholosa. *Felita*. New York: Puffin, 1999. When Felita's family moves to a new neighborhood, her parents promise that she will love it. But her new neighbors tease her because her family is Puerto Rican.

Schecter, Ellen. *The Big Idea*. New York: Hyperion Books for Children, 1996. Eight-year-old Luz hopes to convince her American neighbors to turn a vacant lot into a garden like the garden her grandmother has in Puerto Rico.

NONFICTION

Aliotta, Jerome. *The Puerto Rican Americans*. Chelsea House, 1995. This book covers the struggles of Puerto Rican migrants living on the mainland as they strive for acceptance without giving up their heritage.

Cockcroft, James. *Latino Visions: Contemporary Chicano, Puerto Rican, and Cuban American Artists*. New York: Franklin Watts, 2000. Cockcroft looks at the social and political events that shaped modern Latin American artists, including Puerto Ricans. For older readers.

Johnston, Joyce. *Puerto Rico*. Minneapolis: Lerner Publications Company, 2002. Learn more about Puerto Rico's history and people.

Kaufman, Sheryl Davidson. *Cooking the Caribbean Way.* Minneapolis: Lerner Publications Company, 2002. This book offers cultural information and recipes from Caribbean nations, including Puerto Rico.

Lee, Alfonso Silva. *Coqui y Sus Amigos (Coqui and His Friends).* St Paul, MN: Pangaea, 2000. This book, written in both Spanish and English, offers a look at Puerto Rico's colorful wildlife.

Márquez, Herón. *Latin Sensations.* Minneapolis: Lerner Publications Company, 2001. This book offers brief biographies of several popular Latin American singers, including Ricky Martin and Jennifer Lopez.

Mohr, Nicholasa. *All for the Better: A Story of El Barrio.* Austin, TX: Raintree Steck-Vaughn, 1993. This book tells the story of Evelina Lopez Antonetty, a leader in the New York Puerto Rican community.

Schwabacher, Martin. *Puerto Rico.* New York: Marshall Cavendish, 2001. Read more about the island of Puerto Rico.

Walker, Paul Robert. *Pride of Puerto Rico: The Life of Roberto Clemente.* New York: Harcourt Brace, 1998. This biography covers the life of the legendary Puerto Rican baseball player.

WEBSITES

BORICA.COM
<http://www.boricua.com/>
This website features links to Puerto Rican news and cultural events on both the island and the mainland.

INAMERICABOOKS.COM
<http://www.inamericabooks.com>
Visit www.inamericabooks.com, the on-line home of the In America series, to get linked to all sorts of useful information. You'll find historical and cultural websites related to individual groups as well as general information on genealogy, creating your own family tree, and the history of immigration in America.

WELCOME TO PUERTO RICO
<http://welcometopuertorico.org>
This website features information about the culture and people of Puerto Rico.

INDEX

adaptation to the mainland, 5, 26–27, 30, 32–35, 37–39, 43–44, 55, 57

ASPIRA, 39

Badillo, Herman, 58
Betances, Ramón Emeterio, 16
bodegas, 41, 42
Brooke, John R., 18

Campos, Pedro Albizu, 21
Carib, 9–10, 12–14
citizenship, 5, 7, 19, 20, 35, 44, 48, 50, 53
Clemente, Roberto, 58
Coalition in Defense of Puerto Rican and Hispanic Rights, 50
Columbus, Christopher, 4, 10, 12
compadrazgo, 35
contributions of Puerto Ricans, 5
Cruz, Victor Hernández, 34
cultural differences, 5, 26–27, 30
customs and traditions, 5, 34–35, 41, 43, 45, 46, 48–49

de León, Ponce, 10–12
del Toro, Benicio, 58
discrimination against Puerto Ricans, 5, 26–27, 32, 39, 48, 55

education, 32, 39–40, 52, 55
El Barrio, 36–37, 40, 41, 43
employment, 5, 30–32, 34, 48, 52

families, 33–36, 43, 55
Figueroa, Orlando, 58–59
food, 46–47; recipe, 47
Foraker Act, 18

gangs, 32–33; Young Lords, 33
Gutierrez, Luis, 51

hermandades, 25
housing, 20, 27, 33, 36–37, 40, 54

Institute of Puerto Rican Culture, 38

jibaros, 15
Jones Act, 19–20

language, 5, 27, 30, 32, 34–35, 39, 44–46, 48–49, 52–53, 55
leaders, Puerto Rican: Muñoz Marín, Luis, 22; Muñoz Rivera, Luis, 17
Liga Puertorriqueña, 38
literature, 48, 56
Lopez, Jennifer, 56, 59
Luciano, Felipe, 37

maps, 13, 24
marriage, 14, 34, 35, 55
Martin, Ricky, 59
migrants, Puerto Rican: adaptation of, 5, 26–27, 30, 32–35, 37–39, 43–44, 55, 57; contributions of, 5, 58–61; discrimination against, 5, 26–27, 32, 39, 48, 55; gangs, 32–33; identity, 43–45, 57; nationalist movement, 28–29; numbers of, 5, 26, 48–50, 53; in politics, 5, 17, 33, 44, 50–51, 53
migration, Puerto Rican, 17, 21; to the mainland, 5, 22; history of, 4; reasons for, 5, 20–22, 24, 50; World War II, 22–23
Miles, Nelson, 18
Morales, Aurora Levins, 48
Moreno, Rita, 59
Muñoz Marín, Luis, 22
Muñoz Rivera, Luis, 17

National Congress for Puerto Rican Rights, 50

nationalist movement, 21, 28–29
National Puerto Rican Day Parade,
    38–39, 53, 54, 65
National Puerto Rican Forum
    (NPRF), 37–38
New York City, 5, 17, 21, 23–24, 26,
    30–33, 35–36; El Barrio, 36–37, 40,
    41, 43
Novello, Antonia, 60
Nuyoricans, 44–46, 49, 52–53, 56

Office of the Commonwealth, 24–25,
    50
Operation Bootstrap, 23

Perez, Rosie, 60
political involvement, 5, 17, 33, 44,
    50–51, 53; representation in
    United States, 44, 50, 51
poverty: on the mainland, 27, 35–37,
    40, 54–55; in Puerto Rico, 14, 15,
    18, 19, 20, 21, 22, 50
Puente, Tito, 56, 60
Puerto Rican Association for
    Community Affairs, 38
Puerto Rican Family Institute, 38
Puerto Rican Forum, 38
Puerto Rican Merchants Association,
    38
Puerto Rico: agriculture, 9, 11–12, 14,
    19; Arawak, 8; Carib, 9–10, 12–14;
    Columbus, Christopher, 10, 12;
    as commonwealth of the U.S., 7,
    25, 51; de León, Ponce, 10–12;
    economy, 14–16, 18–23, 50;
    geography, 6–7; independence,
    15–17; jibaros, 15; location, 6;
    military importance, 13; naming
    of, 10, 12; native population, 7–
    10, 14; nickname, 6; religion, 9;
    slavery, 12, 14–16; smallpox, 12;
    Spanish–American War, 17; as
    Spanish colony, 10–17; Taino, 9,

11–12, 14–15; as U.S. possession,
    18–19

recipe, 47
religion, 9, 41
Rodriguez, Abraham, Jr., 60–61
Rodriguez, Juan "Chi Chi," 61

Sanromá, Jesús María, 61
Santiago, Esmeralda, 55, 61
slavery, 12, 14–16
Spanglish, 46, 48
Spanish–American War, 17
statehood, 51

Taino, 9, 11–12, 14–15
Thomas, Piri, 27, 56, 61

United States: conflict over Vieques
    Island, 57; relations with Puerto
    Rico, 7, 17, 18–20, 21, 23, 25, 51

Vasquez, Blanca, 43
Velazquez, Nydia, 51–52
Vieques Island, 6; conflict with
    United States over, 57

welfare, 27

Young Lords, 33

ACKNOWLEDGMENTS: THE PHOTOGRAPHS IN THIS BOOK ARE REPRODUCED WITH THE PERMISSION OF: © Digital Vision, pp. 1, 3, 22; © Suzanne Murphy–Larronde, p. 6; © Dave G. Houser/CORBIS, pp. 7, 57; © Vanni Archive/CORBIS, p.8; Puerto Rico General Archives, pp. 9, 17, 20; Knights of Columbus Headquarters Museum, p. 10; © Brown Brothers, pp. 11, 31, 59 (bottom); Library of Congress, pp. 15 [LC–USF34–012564–E], 16, 33 [LC–USZC2–3682]; © Bettmann/CORBIS, pp. 25, 28, 29, 58 (bottom); © Royalty–Free/CORBIS, p. 26; Museum of the City of New York, p. 36; The Jesús Colón Papers, Centro de Estudios Puertorriqueños, Hunter College, CUNY, p. 38; The Records of the Offices of the Government of Puerto Rico in the U.S., Centro de Estudios Puertorriqueños, Hunter College, CUNY, p. 39; © Frances M. Roberts, pp. 42, 55; © Christopher Felver/CORBIS, p. 45; © Stephanie Maze/CORBIS, p. 48; Office of Congresswoman Nydia Velazquez, p. 52; © Bolivar Arellano/N.Y. Post/CORBIS SYGMA, p. 53; © Nigel N. Elcock, p. 26; Herman Badillo, p. 58 (top); © Frank Trapper/CORBIS, pp. 58 (center), 59 (center), 60 (left); © Daniel Aguilar/ Reuters NewMedia Inc./CORBIS, p. 59 (top); © CORBIS, p. 60 (right); PGA Tour, p. 61 (top); Festival Casals, p. 61 (bottom); Maps by Bill Hauser, pp. 13, 24.

Cover photography by AP/Wide World (top); © Suzanne Murphy–Larronde (bottom); © Digital Vision (title, back cover).